Insurance Planning

Safeguarding Your Wealth and Well-being

Table of Contents

Chapter 1. Introduction

Navigating the labyrinth of insurance planning can often feel like a complex quest, reserved for the financially savvy or risk analysts. However, our special report, "Insurance Planning: Safeguarding Your Wealth and Well-being" seeks to debunk this myth. Written in plain, approachable language, this comprehensive guide takes you on a step-by-step journey to understanding the crucial role insurance planning can play in safeguarding your hard-earned wealth and maintaining your family's well-being. From exploring diverse coverage types to untangling policy fine prints, this report is your tangible key to unlock the world of insurance, transforming it from an intimidating monster into a reliable tool for financial security. With our special report, you'll find, making informed insurance decisions need not be daunting; it can be empowering and exciting. Ready to feel reassured, protected, and in control of your wealth? Let's begin this vital journey in insurance planning.

Chapter 2. Insurance Basics: Know the Fundamentals

Let's begin our journey by understanding the fundamentals. If we liken insurance planning to constructing a building, then understanding the basics of insurance is like laying the foundation. It's crucial, as the rest of your insurance planning will pivot around it. This chapter aims to answer some integral questions - What is insurance? What types are there? Why is it crucial?

2.1. What is Insurance?

Insurance is a unique financial vehicle, a contract (commonly referred to as the 'policy') that you sign up with an insurance company. This agreement states that in the event of specific incidents or risks, the insurance company will compensate you or cover the costs involved. These incidents or 'risks' could range from damage to your home, the onset of a health condition, to even untimely death. In simple words, insurance is a risk management tool that offers financial protection against unforeseen circumstances.

You, as the policyholder, pay a periodic amount, known as a premium, towards the insurance pool. This pool of funds is used to compensate policyholders who incur losses. Insurance operates on the principle of risk pooling where the risk of a single individual is spread across many, making it manageable and economically feasible.

2.2. Types of Insurance

There are a plethora of insurance types available, designed to cover a wide variety of risks. Let's deep-dive to understand some essential insurance types.

2.2.1. Life Insurance

Life insurance protects the financial interests of the policyholder's family and dependents should the insured meet with an untimely death. The policyholder's nominees receive a lump sum, known as the death benefit. Some life insurance policies also offer a savings component, ensuring a maturity amount if the policyholder survives the policy term.

2.2.2. Health Insurance

Health insurance offers coverage for an array of medical expenses, including hospitalization, outpatient procedures, medication, and sometimes even preventive care. Given the skyrocketing healthcare costs, it's a type of policy that is of paramount importance. It ensures that healthcare costs don't deplete one's savings.

2.2.3. Property and Casualty Insurance

Property and casualty insurance is specifically designed to protect physical assets like your home, car, or commercial property. This type of insurance covers costs arising from damage to your assets due to incidents such as fire, theft, natural disasters, or accidents.

2.2.4. Disability Insurance

Disability insurance offers income protection, should one become unable to work because of an illness or injury. It ensures a continuous stream of income, thereby securing one's financial commitments and lifestyle.

2.2.5. Liability Coverage

Liability coverage, typically a part of auto and homeowners' insurance policies, provides protection if the insured is held legally responsible for another person's injury or property damage.

2.2.6. Long-Term Care Insurance

This type of insurance offers coverage for services that help meet your personal or health care needs during a prolonged illness or disability.

2.3. The Importance of Insurance

Understanding why insurance is essential can further deepen your awareness of its indispensability in financial planning.

2.3.1. Financial Protection

Insurance provides financial protection by covering unexpected and often hefty expenses arising from one's life risks. In terms of its payoff, it offers peace of mind and prevents the erosion of your savings due to unforeseen circumstances.

2.3.2. Planning for Life's Stages

Getting the right insurance at the right life stage can help in achieving financial goals while also enduring life's uncertainties. For instance, a newly married couple may invest in life insurance to safeguard their financial future, while a family with elderly members may find health insurance particularly beneficial.

2.3.3. Business Continuity

For businesses, insurance ensures continuity in the face of calamities. It proves particularly valuable for small and medium-size enterprises, where resources are typically limited.

2.3.4. Legal Requirements

Some insurances are legally mandated, like auto insurance in most countries, or professional indemnity insurance for certain professions. Thus, having relevant insurance not only provides financial security but also keeps you legally compliant.

To conclude, comprehension of insurance basics is the stepping stone to smart insurance planning. It empowers you to explore the myriad of insurance policies in the market, understand their relevance to your specific contexts, and consequently make informed choices. The journey may seem exhausting, filled with jargon and technical details, but remember, the time and effort spent in understanding and choosing the right insurance are minuscule compared to the financial and emotional stress it can save you in times of distress. So, no matter where you are in your life journey, consider this as your friendly push towards taking charge of your financial well-being with the right insurance planning.

Chapter 3. Types of Insurance: Exploring Your Options

Every financial journey begins with a single step, and the same applies to exploring insurance. When you initially dive into the world of insurance, you'll discover an imposing array of coverage types, each with its unique advantages, relevance, and complexities. In this chapter, we will unpack the key types of insurance products, providing you an overview of each and guiding you towards the right insurance planning path.

3.1. Life Insurance

Life insurance is an essential part of any sound financial plan. Essentially, it provides your beneficiaries with a sum of money if you pass away during the policy's term. Various types of life insurance exist, including term life insurance, whole life insurance, and universal life insurance.

- **Term Life Insurance**: This is the simplest and typically the cheapest form. In essence, it pays out if the insured person dies within a specified term. However, it has no cash value if the insured person survives the term.

- **Whole Life Insurance**: Unlike term insurance, whole life policies do not expire – they are intended to protect individual for the entire life. They combine insurance with investment, as part of the payment funds the guaranteed death benefit, and the rest is invested.

- **Universal Life Insurance**: A more flexible option, allowing policyholders to alter premium payments and death benefits, and has a cash value component that can grow over time.

Remember, when choosing a life insurance policy, consider your financial situation, age, and the needs of your dependents.

3.2. Health Insurance

Health insurance is a crucial coverage type that assists in paying for medical, surgical, and sometimes dental expenses incurred by the insured. Health insurance can reimburse the insured for expenses due to illness or injury, or pay the care provider directly.

There are several types of health insurance plans:

- **Preferred Provider Organization (PPO)**: Offers both in-network and out-of-network care, with lower costs if you use providers inside the network.

- **Health Maintenance Organization (HMO)**: Covers care only within its network of providers, often needing a referral from a primary care physician for specialist care.

- **High-Deductible Health Plans**: These have higher deductibles but lower premiums and are often paired with Health Savings Accounts that let you pay certain medical expenses with pre-tax money.

Remember, everyone's health circumstances are different, so it's crucial to choose a plan tailored to your needs.

3.3. Homeowner's Insurance

Your home may likely be one of the most substantial financial investments you'll make, and homeowner's insurance helps protect that investment. Homeowner's insurance typically covers damage or destruction to your home and belongings due to a wide range of perils: fire, storm, theft, and others. It can also provide liability coverage if someone is injured on your property.

Two primary types of homeowner's insurance policies are:

- **HO-3**: The most common policy type, covering your home and personal belongings from 16 listed perils.

- **HO-5**: Provides more comprehensive coverage, protecting against any damage unless explicitly out.

3.4. Auto Insurance

Auto insurance safeguards you against financial loss if you have an accident. It's a contract where you pay a premium in return for the insurance company's commitment to pay your vehicle-related losses as outlined in your policy. Auto insurance provides property, liability, and medical coverage:

- **Property coverage**: For damage to, or theft of, your car.

- **Liability coverage**: For your legal responsibility to others for bodily harm or property damage.

- **Medical coverage**: For the cost of treating injuries, rehabilitation, and sometimes lost wages or funeral expenses.

Remember, most states require a minimum amount of auto insurance. However, the minimum is usually inadequate, so consider purchasing more than the statutory minimum.

3.5. Disability Insurance

Despite not being as widely understood or utilized, disability insurance is a significant type of coverage. It provides you with income if an injury or illness prevents you from working. Types of disability insurance include short-term disability, long-term disability, and social insurance disability benefits.

- **Short-term disability** typically covers 60-70 percent of your base salary for a period up to six months.

- **Long-term disability** steps in once the short-term benefits are exhausted, covering 40-60 percent of your base salary.

Disability insurance is crucial if you wouldn't be able to make ends meet if you didn't have income for an extended period.

Exploring the different types of insurance can feel overwhelming, but it helps to remember that you don't have to figure everything out at once. Start by gauging your needs and which types of insurance meet those needs. Once you understand these basics, you'll be better equipped to discuss your options with an insurance adviser and make a choice that best suits your individual circumstances. It's your wealth and well-being on the line, after all. Insurance planning isn't just another item on your to-do list; it's about giving yourself peace of mind and securing your financial future.

Chapter 4. Risk Assessment: Steering Your Safety Net

The first stepping stone on this journey is understanding the concept of risk assessment. While the term 'risk' can elicit a host of negative images, in the context of insurance, it merely represents the financial estimation of potential harm, loss, or damage that could befall you, a family member, or your property.

4.1. Understanding Risk

Risk is an intrinsic part of life, casting its unassuming shadow on every decision, action, or lack of action. In essence, risk comes into play every time we anticipate an outcome but cannot guarantee it. In the domain of insurance, these 'risks' surface as potential situations where you might require additional financial support.

When it comes to penning down all the imaginable risks against your wealth or well-being, the list could be infinite. To have an effective insurance safety net, we would want it to cover those risks which might have a likely likelihood and a significant impact. This is where risk assessment steps in.

Risk assessment, a systemic process of identifying, evaluating, and prioritizing risks, is your trailblazing tool as you weave your way through labyrinthine insurance planning. It empowers you to combat uncertainties with informed financial defenses. This, in turn, ensures that even if a risk evolves into a tangible threat, your wealth and well-being remain cushioned against its jolts.

4.2. Components of Risk Assessment

Risk assessment doesn't require you to carry the weight of a crystal ball. Instead, it demands a clear understanding of your situation and a rigorous yet straightforward methodology. This methodology can broadly be divided into three steps:

1. Risk Identification

2. Risk Evaluation

3. Risk Prioritization

Let's plunge into these individual components for a deeper understanding.

4.3. Risk Identification

This is the stage where you sketch out the range of possible risks that might impact you, your loved ones, or your assets. It's imperative to have an exhaustive list, even if some appear unlikely at first sight.

Begin by assessing risks on an individual level. This could include everything from health risks related to prevalent medical conditions in your family, accidental injury probabilities due to your lifestyle or profession, to lifespan-impacting factors likes age, smoking, or obesity. Remember, these risks often unearth the necessity of life and health insurance.

Next, evaluate risks related to your property, be it home, vehicle, or valuable assets. This might encompass damage risks due to natural disasters, theft, accidents, or depreciation. These risks lend weight to your consideration of home, car, or asset insurance.

Finally, consider the broader financial risks such as loss of income due to job loss, market downturns impacting your investments, or risks related to your long-term financial goals, like a secure retirement.

Keep in mind that risk identification is a dynamic process. With changing circumstances, adopted lifestyle adjustments, or external shifts in the environment, new risks might arise while old ones might diminish. Periodically reviewing and updating your risk assessment is crucial to keeping your insurance plans relevant and robust.

4.4. Risk Evaluation

Once you've mapped out the possible risks, it's time to analyze the impact and likelihood of each. An easy way to navigate this is to categorize the risks into high, medium, and low, both in terms of their potential impact and their probability.

Understanding the financial impact considers the maximum potential loss you can incur if the risk occurs. For instance, the loss involved in a critical illness would be significantly higher in comparison to a minor health ailment.

Likelihood, on the other hand, measures how probable it is that the risk will actually occur. If your family has a history of cardiovascular illnesses, the likelihood of critical heart conditions, and thus the necessity of covering it under your health insurance, is higher.

4.5. Risk Prioritization

Here, you juxtapose the impact and likelihood of each risk to determine which ones ought to be prioritized in your insurance planning. Naturally, risks with high likelihood and major impact should take precedence. Simultaneously, risks with lower chances of occurrence but high impact cannot be disregarded entirely, as their materialization might cast catastrophic impressions on your financial health.

Through effective risk prioritization, we capitalize on our limited financial resources by directing them towards insurances covering high-priority risks. It also provides a foundation to categorize risks that could be managed in other ways - through routine savings, for example - thus avoiding unnecessary insurance premiums.

4.6. Risk Assessment and Insurance Planning

Risk assessment is integral in deciding not only the right types of insurance policies you need but also the extent of your coverage, balancing high protection with affordable premiums. It's about understanding where your financial vulnerabilities lie and consciously making decisions to shield them.

Risk isn't scheduled on a calendar. However, thorough risk assessment can ensure that even slight tremors in your financial landscape don't translate into tectonic shifts impacting your wealth or well-being. With risk assessment as the pilot, you're now better equipped to navigate the vast spectrum of insurance options, steering your own safety net.

Chapter 5. Life Insurance: Security for Your Loved Ones

Providing financial security for your loved ones is one of the most calming thoughts amidst the unpredictable nature of life. Life insurance exists as a versatile tool to achieve this peace of mind, standing as a safety net should the unexpected occur.

5.1. What is Life Insurance?

Life insurance is a contract between an individual (policyholder) and an insurance company. In simple terms, the policyholder regularly pays a premium (monthly, quarterly, semi-annually, or annually), and in exchange, the insurer commits to paying a sum of money (death benefit) to the policyholder's designated beneficiaries upon the policyholder's death.

However, life insurance isn't just limited to providing death benefits. It comes in different types – each with its own features and benefits – ranging from those that offer investment components to ones that gather cash value. The key is to understand the different life insurance types in order to maximize the benefits suitable for your needs.

5.2. Types of Life Insurance

There are mainly two types of life insurance: Term Life Insurance and Permanent Life Insurance. Each comes with a unique set of features that can suit an individual's specific needs.

Chapter 6. Term Life Insurance

Term life insurance, the simplest and usually the most affordable type of life insurance, provides coverage for a specific "term" or time period (10, 20, or 30 years typically). If the policyholder dies during the term, the insurer pays the death benefit to the beneficiaries. However, if the policyholder outlives the term, no benefits are paid out. Some term insurance policies can be converted into permanent insurance at the end of the term.

Chapter 7. Permanent Life Insurance

Permanent life insurance offers lifetime coverage and comes in three main subtypes: Whole Life Insurance, Universal Life Insurance, and Variable Life Insurance.

- Whole Life Insurance guarantees a death benefit to beneficiaries. Moreover, a part of your premium also accumulates as cash value over time which you can borrow against.

- Universal Life Insurance allows the policyholder flexibility in premium payments, death benefits, and savings element.

- Variable Life Insurance combines death protection with a savings account that can be invested in stocks, bonds, and money market mutual funds for potential greater returns.

7.1. Why It's Necessary

Life insurance isn't a luxury but a necessity for anyone with immediate family members or dependents. Its essentiality stems from several reasons:

- Income replacement: Life insurance can replace lost income after the death of the breadwinner, supporting the family financially.

- Debt repayment: It can help repay outstanding personal loans, mortgage, car loans, or credit card bills, preventing the family from inheriting debt.

- Education: The death benefit can ensure that your children's education is not compromised.

- Funeral costs: It can cover funeral and burial expenses which, surprisingly, can be quite high.

7.2. How to Choose the Optimal Life Insurance

Choosing life insurance isn't one-size-fits-all. Several factors need consideration:

Chapter 8. Coverage Length

For Term Life Insurance, select a term that covers the years you'll be paying your largest bills and have dependents. For those who want lifelong coverage, Permanent Life Insurance is the choice.

Chapter 9. Cost

Affordability plays a pivotal role. Term Life Insurance is cheaper, while Permanent Life Insurance is expensive due to the cash-value component and lifetime cover.

Chapter 10. Financial Objectives

If your goal is to leave a legacy, consider Permanent Life Insurance. If the purpose is to cover financial responsibilities only, Term Life Insurance may be suitable.

Chapter 11. Health and Lifestyle

Younger and healthier individuals get lower premiums. Lifestyle habits, like smoking, can affect the premium too.

11.1. Understand Different Riders

Riders are add-ons to the basic insurance policy that provide benefits not covered in the core policy. Some popular riders include Critical Illness Rider, Accidental Death Rider, and Disability Income Rider. Examine the riders and select ones that complement your needs.

11.2. Life Insurance as an Investment

Some life insurance types, primarily Permanent, offer an investment component. They build cash value over time that the policyholder can borrow against. Though they come with higher premiums, these policies can act as a tax-deferred investment and enhance your wealth.

11.3. Conclusion

Life insurance is one of the most crucial financial protections you can provide for your loved ones. Understanding different types, knowing when and why to get it, and the process of choosing the best-suited policy for your needs can ensure that you're making the best choice. Life insurance isn't about the end; it's about what continues after.

Chapter 12. Health Insurance: Your Shield against Medical Emergencies

12.1. Understanding Health Insurance

Health insurance is a type of insurance coverage that compensates the insured for medical expenses incurred from illness or injury, or pays the care provider directly. This coverage is a contract between you and your insurer, which stipulates that in exchange for premiums, the insurer will pay for your healthcare expenses which are stipulated in your policy. In essence, it's your financial shield against high and unpredictable healthcare costs.

12.2. Why You Need Health Insurance

One cannot overstate the importance of health insurance in your financial planning. Few of us can predict when we might become ill or get injured, and healthcare costs can quickly add up. Health insurance can help you meet these costs, provide access to better medical care, and offer financial protection not just for you, but also your family.

1. **Unforeseen Medical Costs**: Even relatively minor procedures can come with significant costs. A broken leg can cost many thousands of dollars to treat; a week-long hospital stay can cost tens of thousands. Without health insurance, you would bear these costs yourself.

2. **Preventive Services**: In addition to covering illness and injury treatment, many health insurance plans also cover preventive services. This includes vaccinations, screenings, and well-child visits that can keep you healthy.

3. **Access to a Broad Network of Healthcare Providers**: Health insurers negotiate lower prices with a network of healthcare providers. Insured individuals can access this network and receive treatment at lower out-of-pocket costs than they would otherwise.

4. **Legal Requirement**: In some countries like the U.S., health insurance is a legal requirement, and you may face penalties for not having coverage.

12.3. Types of Health Insurance

There are several types of health insurance, each with its benefits and drawbacks. We'll cover the four most common types: employer-provided, self-purchased, government-provided, and direct primary care.

1. **Employer-Provided Health Insurance**: Many employers offer health insurance as part of their benefits package. These policies often cover the employee and their dependents. Premiums are typically cheaper because employers cover a significant portion.

2. **Self-Purchased Health Insurance**: Individuals who do not receive coverage from an employer or government plan can purchase health insurance independently. This route can often be more expensive but also gives the purchaser more freedom to tailor their coverage.

3. **Government-Provided Health Insurance**: Most countries have some government-provided healthcare, which may be part of a social safety net, or universal healthcare system. This type of insurance often has lower premiums and out-of-pocket costs but longer wait times for procedures.

4. **Direct Primary Care**: This is a relatively new healthcare model that bypasses insurance. Instead, patients pay a monthly fee directly to their doctor for a suite of primary care services.

12.4. Understanding Your Health Insurance Policy

Your insurance policy is a contract between you and your insurer. It contains crucial information about what is covered, what is not, how much you can expect to pay, how to file a claim, and much more. This section is vital, not just for making informed decisions about your healthcare but for ensuring you get the most out of your insurance.

1. **Premiums**: This is the amount you pay for your insurance policy, often billed monthly.

2. **Deductible**: This is what you pay out of pocket before your insurance kicks in.

3. **Copayments and Coinsurance**: These are your share of the cost for services after your deductible. A copayment is a fixed amount; coinsurance is a percentage of the cost.

4. **Out-Of-Pocket Maximum**: This is the most you'll have to pay for covered services in a policy period. After you hit this limit, your insurance will pay for all covered services.

12.5. Choosing the Right Health Insurance

Choosing the right health insurance is a key component in managing unforeseen medical emergencies. There are various aspects to consider when choosing a plan, including premiums, coverage, out-of-pocket costs, and provider networks.

1. **Evaluate your healthcare needs**: Consider your past healthcare usage, your current health status, and any known upcoming healthcare needs.

2. **Compare costs**: Not just premiums, but also potential out-of-pocket costs (including deductibles, copays, and coinsurance).

3. **Check the network of doctors and hospitals**: Ensure they adequately cover your area and include any preferred doctors or specialists.

4. **Look at the list of covered drugs**: If you regularly take certain medications, make sure they are covered.

5. **Consider the quality of the plan**: Check the accreditation and rating of the plan from state or independent rating agencies.

12.6. Conclusion

Navigating the world of health insurance might seem complex and overwhelming, but understanding its basic principles is crucial for safeguarding your health and financial well-being. As an integral part of your financial plan, health insurance can provide peace of mind, knowing you're protected against overwhelming medical costs. Your journey towards a secure future starts with taking the time to understand, research, and select the health insurance plan that best fits your needs, both now and looking to the future. By using this guide, you're taking a step towards becoming an empowered insurance consumer.

Chapter 13. Home and Auto Insurance: Securing Tangible Assets

Home and auto insurance are two of the most common forms of property insurance that protect you against significant monetary losses stemming from damage or theft of your major assets – your home and your car. Our overview of this essential form of coverage aims to guide you in making informed decisions about protecting your important tangible assets.

13.1. Understanding Home and Auto Insurance

At its core, home insurance covers the loss or damage of a person's residential property. In essence, if you are a homeowner, home insurance is a contract between you and your insurance company, wherein the company promises to pay for any serious damages to your home or possessions therein, provided such damages are covered within your policy. Similarly, auto insurance provides coverage against losses incurred as a result of car accidents or theft. Auto coverage includes liability insurance for bodily injury and property damage, coverage for the damage to your own car, and coverage for medical expenses.

A good insurance policy doesn't just protect your home and car; it also protects your lifestyle and in many cases, your personal well-being. For example, if your home is rendered inhabitable due to a covered peril, your policy may often cover your temporary living expenses while repairs are made.

13.2. Types of Coverage

Every insurance policy typically comprises multiple 'coverages'. A coverage essentially refers to a specific eventuality, situation or peril that your insurance policy safeguards you against.

Home insurance typically includes the following types of coverage: * Dwelling coverage: Protects the structure of your home, such as the walls and roof. * Personal property coverage: Protects your personal belongings in your home, such as furniture, clothing, and appliances. * Liability protection: Shields you from being sued for damages or accidental injuries caused by you or your family members. * Additional living expenses (ALE): Covers the cost of living elsewhere if your home becomes inhabitable due to a covered event.

For auto insurance, basic coverage would commonly include: * Liability coverage: Covers expenses related to injury, death or property damage in an accident where you're at fault. * Comprehensive coverage: Protects against damage to your car due to theft, vandalism, or non-collision related incidents. * Collision coverage: Covers damage to your car caused by a collision with another vehicle or object. * Personal injury protection: Covers medical expenses, no matter who is at fault.

13.3. Assessing Your Insurance Needs

When assessing your insurance needs, it's recommended to consider the worst-case scenario. Think about what the potential cost might be if your home was completely destroyed or your car badly damaged. Assessing the worst-case scenario can guide you in selecting coverage limits that align with your financial and risk comfort levels.

When it comes to home insurance, factor in the value of your home and its contents, any potential liability risks you might face, and how much it would cost for you to live in a hotel or a rented place if your home becomes inhabitable. For auto insurance, consider the cost of repairing your car, medical costs for possible accidents, and what you'd be able to pay if you caused an accident that resulted in significant damage or loss to others.

13.4. Reading Your Insurance Policy

Understanding your insurance policy can be a daunting task, given the often complex legal verbiage. But, it's important to remember that your insurance policy is a contract and you should know its terms thoroughly. Look for the limits mentioned in your policy – these are the maximum amounts your insurance provider would pay you. Deductibles, the amount you pay out-of-pocket before insurance kicks in, should also be carefully noted.

13.5. Negotiating Your Premium

Premium is the amount of money you pay for your insurance policy. There are several factors that influence your premium including location, age and condition of your home or car, your own personal claims history, and more. To reduce your premium, consider various ways like bundling home and auto insurance, increasing your deductible, improving your home's safety and security, maintaining a clean driving record, and regularly reviewing your policy and making necessary adjustments.

This chapter aimed at empowering you with a deeper understanding of home and auto insurance so you're armed with the knowledge to make informed decisions. Always remember, the goal of insurance planning is, above all things, to provide you and your family peace of mind and financial security. As you prepare to navigate your unique insurance needs, keep this goal close to your heart.

Understanding and strategizing your insurance plan should serve your personal financial situation and well-being. Begin by looking at the worst-case scenario and slowly gauge your ability to afford that. Then consider how much you are willing to pay for peace of mind, and if there are several discounts and benefits that would be of significant help.

Welcome this journey as an empowering one where your diligent preparations work towards securing your hard-earned tangible assets. Surely, there will be times when you'll feel like you're in a maze, but remember - in the end, the jewel is well worth the adventure.

Chapter 14. Disability and Liability Insurance: A Comprehensive Overview

Disability and liability insurance form the cornerstone of a well-rounded insurance policy portfolio. These specific coverage types protect individuals financially whether a incident inhibits their ability to work or if their actions unintentionally bring harm to others.

14.1. Understanding Disability Insurance

Disability insurance is also known as income protection. But why is it so critical? If you had a money machine at home, you'd probably insure it. You are that money machine. Your capacity to earn is your most considerable asset, and just like any other precious asset, it's worth protecting.

There are two main types of disability insurance: short-term and long-term. Short-term disability insurance usually provides benefits for up to six months, while long-term disability insurance provides benefits for an extended period, often until retirement or for life.

The exact terms of coverage vary by policy, but typically, disability insurance pays a part of your income if an illness or injury prevents you from working. It may also provide for rehabilitation and training.

When considering disability insurance, remember to evaluate your personal risk factors, including your health, lifestyle, and job environment. Accurately understanding your risk empowers you to select a policy that grants you optimum coverage.

14.2. Unraveling Liability Insurance

Liability insurance protects you if you're held legally accountable for injury or property damage to another party. It typically covers legal costs and any necessary payouts. There are several types of liability insurance coverages, including auto, homeowners, renters, and commercial.

Auto liability insurance, for example, is required in most states and covers the cost of damages you cause to others in an auto accident. Homeowners and renters liability insurance, on the other hand, protect you if a guest is injured in your residence or if you cause damage to your rental apartment. Commercial liability insurance protects businesses against claims for injury or property damage resulting from their operations.

Each one of these coverage types offers varying depths of protection, and policy limits are customizable to your specific needs.

14.3. Evaluating Disability and Liability Coverage

Evaluating the right coverage begins with understanding the potential financial risks associated with disability or liability. For disability insurance, consider factors like your age, health, income, and whether you have dependents. Remember, the aim is to replace a significant portion of your income if you're unable to work.

When it comes to liability coverage, evaluate the potential risks in your environment. Do you have a swimming pool or a trampoline? Do you own a dog? These are all potential sources of liability claims.

Always aim for coverage limits that will adequately protect your assets. This is where the assistance of a qualified broker or agent becomes invaluable.

14.4. The Impact of Disability and Liability Claims

It's essential to understand the potential impact of a disability or liability claim on your financial health. A disability can lead to loss of income and increased medical expenses. Meanwhile, a liability claim can result in legal fees and settlements that can amount to hundreds of thousands of dollars. These financial losses can drain savings and retirement funds, and in extreme instances, lead to bankruptcy.

Insurance is more than a business transaction; it's securing peace of mind. By comprehensively understanding disability and liability insurance, you're not only safeguarding your wealth but also guaranteeing the peace of mind that comes with financial security. Protect yourself, shield your assets, and navigate your future with confidence.

14.5. Final Thoughts

Insurance planning, particularly regarding disability and liability insurance, is not about fearing the worst but preparing for the unpredictable. It's about maintaining control over your wealth and well-being, regardless of circumstances. Our hopes are that you utilize this knowledge to make informed decisions leading to the secure and prosperous future you deserve.

Chapter 15. Choosing Your Policy: Navigating the Fine Print

The journey to deciphering the mystery of an insurance policy starts with understanding one critical piece: policy fine print. The fine print or the policy wording is typically where crucial details reside, those that define the terms and conditions, exclusions, and coverage limits. Complex jargon and legal terms often population these sections, making it an intimidating read. However, understanding this fine print is not impossible. With patience and guidance, you too can unravel its intricacies.

15.1. Understanding Policy Wordings

Before delving deep into the specifics, it can be beneficial to develop a general understanding of what the policy document contains. The first thing you should look at is the "Definitions" or the "Glossary," which often appear at the beginning of the document. This section provides meanings to crucial terms used throughout the policy. Once you have a grasp of these terms, reading the remaining sections becomes easier.

Following the definitions, you will typically encounter the "Coverage" section. Here, the policy details what risks it covers and to what extent. You should carefully scrutinize this portion, as it dictates what you are protected against.

Next, there is an "Exclusions" section. This part informs you of the circumstances or conditions that the policy does not cover. For instance, a home insurance policy might exclude damage caused by normal wear and tear or a natural disaster like an earthquake unless specified.

Lastly, the "Conditions and Limitations" section provides details about your obligations as a policyholder and the extent of the coverages. Here you'll find information about limitations on payouts, policy renewability, claim procedures, and more.

Reading through the policy document once will give you a sense of the information it contains, but a thorough review requires a more strategic approach. Here are a few key steps to keep in mind:

15.2. Analyzing the Details

Let's delve into the specifics for policy analysis. You will start with two key chapters: coverage and exclusions.

Check the coverage details meticulously. It's always beneficial to list down the events or risks covered and match them against your needs. For a healthcare policy, check if it covers all the necessary treatments, hospital stays, post-hospital care, medicines, etc. For a car insurance policy, make sure it includes risks you see as relevant - accident, theft, fire, and so on. It's also essential to understand the degree of coverage. Some policies might provide a full cover, while others may only cover a percentage of the costs.

Once you have a clear understanding of the coverage, switch to the exclusions. It's equally important to identify what's not covered typically situated in a separate section or outlined beneath each covered item. Note that some policies may use specific exclusions (for example, "excluding pre-existing medical conditions") while others may employ broad exclusions (like "excluding any condition for which medication, advice, or treatment was recommended or received within a 24-month period before the coverage effective date"). By understanding the exclusions, you can gauge the true protective capability of your policy.

15.3. Reading the Subtle Language

Once you have a lay of the policy landscape, it's crucial to look at some of the subtler language embedded within the policy fine print.

Among this subtle language will be words stipulating conditions, such as "and," "or," "may," "might," "shall", etc. Their use can significantly impact how a policy is interpreted, and hence, may influence claim handling and payouts. For instance, in life insurance policies, words like "may" or "might" hint at conditional situations, which need to be given keen attention.

Also, pay attention to words of limitation. Sentences that use phrases like "up to," "maximum," or "limit" imply there are bounds on the coverage you can receive, which can significantly impact the usefulness of the policy. Understanding these limitations can help you adjust your expectations concerning potential claims and payouts.

15.4. Cancellation, Premiums, and Renewability

Another area of the policy fine print that deserves your attention is the terms surrounding cancellation, premiums, and renewability.

The cancellation clause details the terms and conditions under which the policyholder or the insuring company can terminate the policy. It will list down the circumstances that can lead to cancellation and the associated repercussions.

In terms of premiums, check whether they can increase over the lifespan of the policy. Increased premiums directly affect your financial commitments. Make sure you're comfortable with potential increases, or opt for a policy that guarantees fixed premiums.

Renewability is another crucial factor to focus on. Policies with "guaranteed renewability" can't be canceled by the insurer for health-related reasons and can offer a degree of comfort.

Exploring these three sections will give deeper insight into how flexible and adaptable your policy is to changes in circumstances.

We hope this detailed guideline assists you in successfully navigating the labyrinth of policy fine print. Understanding this fine print will strengthen your grasp on insurance planning, direct you towards making informed decisions, and ultimately safeguard your wealth and well-being. Remember, insurance planning doesn't have to be daunting. With the right knowledge and tools, it can become an exciting journey towards achieving financial security.

Chapter 16. Successful Claim Processing: When the Unexpected Happens

Filing an insurance claim can be stressful, especially when the unexpected happens. But with proper knowledge and preparedness, the process can become both manageable and empowering. Let's dive into the rich trove of information to help you understand claim processing — the whys, the hows, and the expected outcomes.

16.1. Understanding Insurance Claims

An insurance claim is a formal request to an insurance company, asking for a payment based on the terms of the insurance policy. When a claim is made, the insurance company will review the claim for validity, and then either approve or deny it based on their findings. It's important to note that filing a claim is not an instantaneous process — it often involves a series of steps that must be completed to reach a resolution.

16.2. When to File a Claim

Key to a successful claim processing is knowing when to file. Generally, an insurance claim should be filed as soon as an event occurs that leads to loss or damage covered by your insurance policy. Timing is crucial because delayed reporting may complicate the process or even jeopardize your chance of getting the claim approved.

16.3. Preparing for Claim Filing

Preparation is key for an effective claim filing process. Ensure to gather all necessary documents required by your insurance company. This usually includes your personal identification, policy number, and documentation of the loss or damage (e.g., photographs, reports, receipts).

Having all your documentation ready can speed up the process and increase the likelihood of a successful claim, as your insurer can verify the information swiftly.

16.4. The Claim Filing Process

Each insurance company has its own set of procedures for filing a claim. It's essential to contact your insurer as soon as the event happens. They will guide you through their specific process, which typically involves steps like:

1. Outline of the event detailing the when, where, and how everything transpired.

2. Documentation to support your claim.

3. Completion of a claim form.

It's advisable to document each stage and keep records of all communication about the claim, including dates, times, names, and the content of conversations or correspondence.

16.5. The Adjustment Process

Once a claim is filed, an adjuster is assigned to evaluate the claim. They will examine the documentation, carry out investigations if required, and may also visit the location of loss or damage.

Your cooperation with your adjuster can significantly influence the speed and outcome of your claim. Provide any additional documentation they may request promptly to ensure a smooth process.

16.6. Understanding Your Settlement

Understanding how the settlement process works can help you anticipate the outcome of your claim. Settlements can occur in various ways: repair or replacement, cash payment, or a combination. Be clear about your policy details to understand how your insurance company will settle your claim.

16.7. Appealing a Denied Claim

If your claim is denied, or the payout is less than anticipated, you usually have the right to appeal. The appeal process varies by insurance company, but it typically involves submitting additional information or arguing for a reevaluation.

Bear in mind that success in appealing a claim often depends on whether the original denial was due to lack of documentation or differing interpretations of the coverage.

16.8. Conclusion

There's no denying that filing an insurance claim can be a complex process. It's often filled with unfamiliar terms and procedures. However, armed with an understanding of the process and a readiness to actively participate in settling your claim, you can transform the claim filing task from a mystery to a corner piece in your wealth and well-being safeguard puzzle.

Remember, the ultimate goal of insurance is to return you to the financial state before the loss or damage happened. With patience, and sound knowledge, successfully processing an insurance claim can become an achievable task rather than an overwhelming challenge.

Creating an open line of communication with your insurer, understanding your policy's specifications, and arming yourself with all required documents will smooth your claim process journey. A successful claim process is not only a sign of effective insurance planning but also a testimony to your resilience and readiness in the face of unexpected events.

With this knowledge, may your claim journey be successful, empowering you to face the unexpected with assurance, knowing that you are protected and in command.

Chapter 17. Insurance Planning as Part of Wealth Management: An Integrated Approach

Insurance planning operates within the larger context of wealth management, playing an integral and pivotal role in protecting and multiplying the financial resources of individuals and families. It is indubitably a cog in the financial planning wheel and sits at the confluence of risk management, financial stability and capital growth.

17.1. Understanding the Rationale: Why Insurance is Essential in Wealth Management

Wealth is not an end in itself but a means to an end - that of a secure, comfortable and stress-free life. Insurance is fundamental to wealth management in that it provides certainty in uncertain times, acting as a bulwark against unforeseen eventualities, calamities, and losses. Whether it's helping keep family finances afloat during sudden job loss, helping maintain certain lifestyle standards despite rising healthcare costs, or ensuring that your family's dreams live on after you're no longer around, insurance enables you, in no uncertain terms, to weather life's storms.

Moreover, with the right insurance plans, you also have a potent tool for creating wealth. Certain life insurance plans come with dual benefits of protection and long-term investment opportunities, helping you inch towards financial goals while offering life cover.

17.2. The Building Blocks: Types of Insurance in Wealth Management

Integral to wealth management are various types of insurances that protect different facets of your financial health. Here are some premier insurance types that work towards wealth preservation:

-Life Insurance: This primary protection must-have pays a lump sum to your family upon your death or disability, thereby preventing financial hardship.

-Health Insurance: Given escalating treatment costs, health insurance helps manage medical expenses and ensures good healthcare is never compromised.

-Property Insurance: It safeguards valuable possessions like your home and car against damages from contingencies like theft or natural disasters.

-Disability Insurance: By replacing lost income owing to a disability, this insurance shields your income stream.

-Critical Illness Insurance: This insurance comes in handy to cover expenses for grave diseases that are not commonly included in conventional health insurance.

Moreover, a prudent wealth manager will recommend a mix of traditional and Unit Linked Insurance Plans (ULIPs). While traditional plans focus on guaranteed returns, ULIPs, with their equity exposure, can aid in wealth creation.

17.3. Navigating Diverse Coverage Types

Navigating through the expanse of insurance coverages can be daunting. Here's a closer look at the various options:

-Whole Life Insurance: This offers life-long coverage and usually incorporates a cash value element.

-Term Life Insurance: It provides coverage for a specified term and pays benefits only if the insured dies during that term.

-Universal Life Insurance: This is a more flexible version of Whole Life Insurance where premium payments above the cost of insurance are credited to the cash value.

-Variable Life Insurance: Here, the cash value can be invested in a selection of sub-accounts similar to mutual funds, equities, or bonds.

Choosing the appropriate coverage type depends on factors like financial goals, risk appetite, life stage, and personal situation. It requires meticulous planning and expert advice for optimal benefits.

17.4. Connecting the Dots: Harmonizing Insurance and Wealth Management

Implementing insurance as part of wealth management is a multi-step process:

-Assess Risk: Evaluate your risk exposure based on areas like occupation, health, assets, lifestyle, and liabilities.

-Determine Goals: Define what you hope to achieve long-term

through insurance coverage.

-Choose Insurance Type and Plan: Select insurance types and coverage that align best with your risk assessment and goals.

-Regular Review: Review your plan periodically to ensure it remains adequate, relevant, and responsive to your changing needs and goals.

Insurance doesn't exist in a vacuum; it needs to be synched with your overall financial planning and aligned with your financial goals. Consequently, integrating it with investment strategy, tax planning, retirement planning and estate planning is crucial for an encompassing wealth management plan.

17.5. Decoding the Fine Print: understanding Policy Terms

Every insurance contract comes with its set of terms and conditions. Understanding and assessing these diligently prevents unpleasant surprises later. Here are a few quintessential terms to consider:

-Premium: The amount you pay for insurance coverage.

-Sum Assured: The agreed-upon amount the insurance company will pay upon the occurrence of an insured event.

-Policy Term: Refers to the number of years the insurance plan is effective.

-Life Assured: The person on whose life the insurance plan is drafted.

To conclude, insurance planning is an indispensable part of comprehensive wealth management. It provides an essential safety net for your wealth and well-being, buffering you against financial shocks arising from unforeseen events. With a robust insurance plan in place, you can confidently endeavor to fulfill life goals and ambitions, secure in the knowledge that your wealth is not merely well-managed, but well-protected too.